Just Like Me

Mary J. Davis

These pages may be copied.
Permission is granted to the buyer of this book to
photocopy student materials for use with
Sunday school or Bible teaching classes.

For information regarding the CPSIA on this printed material call:
203-595-3636 and provide reference # LANC-315751

rainbowpublishers®

Rainbow Publishers • P.O. Box 261129 • San Diego, CA 92196
www.RainbowPublishers.com

With thanks to Rainbow Publishers for allowing me to do what I love to do most in writing Christian materials for the glory of God.

Instant Bible Lessons for Nursery: Just Like Me
©2012 by Rainbow Publishers
ISBN 10: 1-58411-120-8
ISBN 13: 978-1-58411-120-7
Rainbow reorder# RB38712
RELIGION / Christian Ministry / Children

Rainbow Publishers
P.O. Box 261129
San Diego, CA 92196
www.RainbowPublishers.com

Cover Illustrator: Stacey Lamb
Interior Illustrator: Jon Mitchell

SUSTAINABLE FORESTRY INITIATIVE
Certified Chain of Custody
At Least 20% Certified Forest Content
www.sfiprogram.org
SFI-00484

Printed in the United States of America

Contents

Introduction 5

How to Use This Book 5

Chapter 1: Jesus was a Baby, Just Like Me 7

Story to Share..7

Story Poster 8

Nativity Play Set 10

Just Like Me Song 12

Rock-a-Bye Rhyme................................13

Jesus is Born Story Book 14

Easy Ornament.....................................17

Praising Baby Jesus Puzzle 18

Chapter 2: Jesus Loved God's House, Just Like Me 19

Story to Share.......................................19

Story Poster 20

Inside God's House Folding Picture Book 22

Let Us Go to the House of the Lord Song....24

I Love God's House Action Rhyme 25

Stained Glass Church Windows 26

House of the Lord Collage 27

Welcome Sign...28

Chapter 3: Jesus Had Friends, Just Like Me 29

Story to Share.......................................29

Story Poster 30

Lollipop Puppets...................................32

Come Follow Me Song 33

Footprints Plaque.................................34

Friends Make Me Happy Picture 35

Hide and Seek Friends 36

Chapter 4: Jesus Loved God's Word, Just Like Me 37

Story to Share..37

Story Poster 38

Bible Bookmark 40

My Bible Song...41

God's Word Action Rhyme......................42

I Love God's Word Coloring Book 43

Hidden Pictures Puzzle.....................................45

Chapter 5: Jesus Liked to Help, Just Like Me 47

Story to Share..47

Story Poster 48

What Helpers Use Puzzle 50

Jesus Helped Song 55

Story Ball 52

Hand-Shape Book 54

Chapter 6: Jesus Loves Others, Just Like Me 57

Story to Share..57

Story Poster 58

Love Others Sun Catchers 60

Love One Another Song..........................61

Soft Heart Rattles 62

Love One Another Puzzle 63

Show My Love Action Rhyme 64

Heart Bubble Wands...............................65

I Love You Handprint 66

Chapter 7: Jesus Told Others About God, Just Like Me 67

Story to Share..67

Story Poster 68

Telling Friends About God Song 70

Hear About God Action Rhyme 71

Double Story Book..................................72

Telling About God Phone 75

Tell Others Coloring Picture to Share 76

Chapter 8: Jesus Prayed to God, Just Like Me 77

Story to Share..................................77

Story Poster......................................78

Praying Song Poster 80

Prayer Plaque..................................81

Prayer Cards 82

Chapter 9: More Just Like Me Activities.....................................85

Bulletin Board Border....................86

Easy Puzzle 88

Just Like Me Picture Book..............91

Attendance Chart............................96

Introduction

The nursery is a wonderful place to start the Christian education of children. Whether they are infants or older babies, children can learn that Jesus' life was, in many ways, just like their own lives. Post many pictures of Jesus on walls, bulletin boards or under a see-through mat on the floor. Make Jesus the focus of every class time.

The lessons in *Instant Bible Lessons for Nursery: Just Like Me* include Bible stories about events in Jesus' life that also relate the story to a young child's life. Teachers can tell Bible stories, say the memory verse and present activities that will appeal to a variety of nursery-aged children. If your nursery has only babies one week, use the story poster ideas and sing the verse songs many times during class. Older babies will enjoy the crafts and touchable activities. Some of the crafts and games may seem a little old for babies, but the children will enjoy 'helping' as much as they can. In all cases, the teacher can repeat the story and memory verses for great one-on-one activities.

You may send story posters, rhyme pages and many other activities from this book home with parents so they may continue the lesson theme throughout the week.

Get ready to have fun in the nursery!

✳ How to Use This Book ✳

Each chapter begins with a Bible story which you may read to your class or to a child one-on-one. The questions after each lesson can be used as an opportunity for you to continue telling the story. Ask and answer each question for the children. Encourage older babies to repeat some of the words of the story or memory verse with you.

Every story chapter includes a bulletin board poster with the memory verse and suggestions for using the poster as an activity. All activities are tagged with one of the icons below so you can quickly flip through the chapter and select the projects you need. Simply cut off the teacher instructions on the pages and duplicate.

Chapter 1

Jesus was a Baby, Just like Me

Memory Verse

And he gave him the name Jesus. ~Matthew 1:25

Story to Share

An angel came to Mary and said, "You will have a special baby. He is God's Son. Give Him the name Jesus."

Then an angel came to Joseph and said, "Mary will have a baby boy. He is God's Son. Give Him the name Jesus."

Mary and Joseph had to take a long trip to Bethlehem. When they got there Joseph asked around for a nice room and soft bed for Mary. But there were no rooms in the city. Joseph and Mary went to a stable to sleep. There, Mary's baby was born. Mary wrapped Him in cloths and placed Him in a manger. They gave Him the name Jesus.

Angels appeared to shepherds in the field. The angels sang and praised God, singing, "Glory to God. We bring you good news of great joy. A baby, the Christ, has been born. You will find Him wrapped in cloths and lying in a manger." The shepherds hurried to find baby Jesus and worship Him.

The angels praised God. The shepherds worshipped God's Son. What a wonderful gift to us: a Savior named Jesus.

~Based on Matthew 1:18-25; Luke 1:26-38; 2:1-20

Story Review

1. Who told Mary she would have a baby? An angel told Mary she would have a baby.

2. Who told Joseph that Mary would have a baby? An angel told Joseph that Mary would have a baby.

3. Whose son is baby Jesus? Baby Jesus is God's Son.

Parent Corner

1. Let your baby touch the pieces from a nativity scene. Say the names **Joseph**, **Mary** and **Jesus**. If your nativity scene contains animals and/or angels, name them also. Say, **Jesus was a little baby, just like you.**

2. Show your baby a picture of him/herself and also a picture of baby Jesus (the one in the story poster will work). Say, **Jesus was a little baby. Here is baby Jesus. You are (were) a little baby. Here is a picture of you. Jesus was a little baby, just like you.**

Bulletin Board

What You Need

- pattern on page 9
- clear adhesive-backed plastic
- stickers of angels, lambs, donkeys or cattle

What To Do

1. Depending on how you want to use the poster (see ideas below), enlarge, reduce or simply copy page 9 to fit your bulletin board space.

2. To make a take-home paper duplicate the story page to the back of story poster.

3. To use the poster as an in-class activity help the children place some angel stickers or lamb, donkey and cattle stickers on the page.

Story Poster

▭▭▷ Poster Pointer

Fasten a poster on the wall above the diaper station/changing table. Put another poster on a table close to the rocking chair. Use poster for one-on-one time with babies. Tell the Bible story or say the memory verse many times during nursery time.

And he gave him the name Jesus.

~Matthew 1:25

HaNdS ON

what you Need

- pages 10 and 11, duplicated
- five paper or plastic cups for each nativity set
- scissors
- glue

what To Do

1. Before class, cut out the five picture squares from the two pattern pages. Turn five paper or plastic cups upside down. Glue one picture square onto each of the five paper or plastic cups.

2. Set the five nativity cups on a table or play mat. Let each baby touch each one and help them place the cups in a group while you retell the story.

3. Say, **Jesus was a baby, just like you.**

Baby

⚬❀☊ Nativity Play Set ☊❀⚬

finished craft

♪♫ Song

What You Need
- duplicated page

What To Do
1. Sing the song to the tune of "I'm a Little Teapot."
2. Hold each baby and rock him/her on your knee as you sing the song again.

Just Like Me Song

Jesus was a baby, just like me.

Our mommies rocked us on their knee.

Jesus was a special gift from God.

I am special, I show God's love.

Baby

Rock-a-Bye Rhyme

Rock-a-bye little baby Jesus

Rock-a-bye God sent you.

Rock-a-bye little baby Jesus

Rock-a-bye God sent you.

Rock-a-bye little baby [baby's name]

Rock-a-bye God loves you.

Rock-a-bye little baby [baby's name]

Rock-a-bye God loves you.

Rhyme

What You Need
- duplicated page
- crayons

What To Do
1. Hold each baby and rock him/her while you say the rhyme.
2. Older babies will enjoy coloring the pictures on the page.

Baby

Read to Me

What You Need
- pages 14, 15 and 16, duplicated to card stock
- hole punch
- plastic rings

What To Do
1. Before class, duplicate the three pages to card stock. Cut the cover from the instruction page. Cut the other two pages apart on the bold lines. Put the six pages together in order. Punch two or three holes in the left side of the book. Fasten the book together with plastic rings.
2. Hold each baby while you read the book out loud. Let children touch the book pages while you read.

Baby

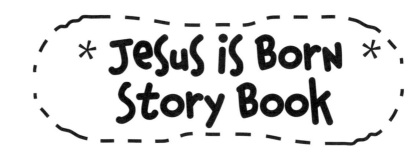

Jesus was a Baby, Just Like Me

Mary and Joseph went on a long trip to Bethlehem. Mary was tired. But, there was no room in any inn.

Joseph found a stable for Mary to rest in. Mary's baby was born in the stable. She wrapped him in cloths and placed him in a manger. They called him Jesus.

An angel told Mary she would have a baby boy. He would be God's Son. The angel said, "Give him the name Jesus."

An angel visited Joseph in a dream. The angel said, "Mary will have a baby boy. He is God's Son. Give him the name Jesus."

Angels sang praises to God. An angel told the shepherds in the field, "I bring you good news of great joy!"

The shepherds hurried to see God's Son, baby Jesus. Angels praised God. Shepherds praised God. Mary and Joseph praised God.

Easy Ornament

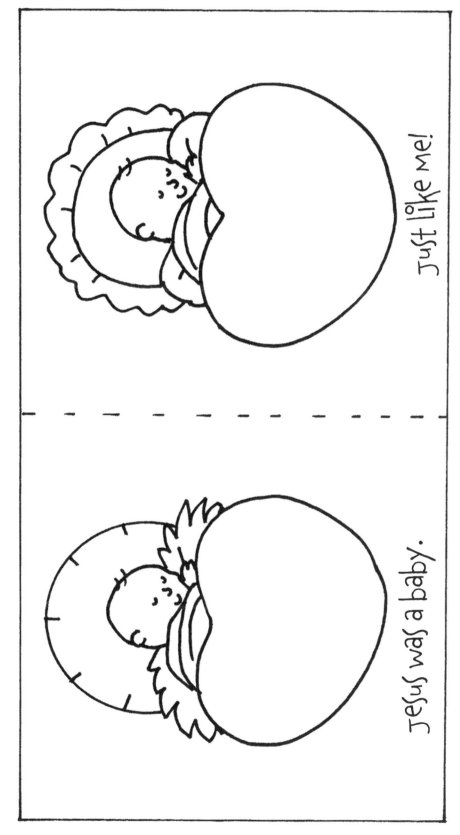

Just like me!

Jesus was a baby.

Easy Craft

What You Need
- duplicated page for each child
- scissors
- tape
- yarn
- crayons
- pretzel twists
- glue

What To Do
1. Before class, cut and fold an ornament for each child. Tape the bottom of the ornament to hold it closed. Tape a loop of yarn at top to hang.
2. Read both sides of the ornament to the baby. Show the baby how to point to Jesus, then to the baby on the opposite side. Call the baby in the picture by the child's name.
3. Let older babies color the ornament.
4. Help each baby glue a pretzel twist inside each of the blank areas under each baby to form a manger/crib.

Baby

Puzzle

Praising Baby Jesus Puzzle

what you Need
• duplicated page for each child
• crayons

what To Do
1. Help each child trace the broken lines with a crayon or finger to help each shepherd find baby Jesus.
2. Say, **The angels told the shepherds that God's Son was born in Bethlehem. Trace the lines to help each shepherd find baby Jesus.**
3. Older babies may enjoy coloring the picture.

Baby

Chapter 2

Jesus Loved God's House, Just Like Me

Memory Verse

Let us go to the house of the Lord. ~Psalm 122:1

 ## Story to Share

Mary and Joseph took Jesus on a long trip to God's house in Jerusalem. When they started on the trip home Mary and Joseph didn't know Jesus wasn't with them. After a while they began to look for Jesus. He was just a boy. Where could he be?

They traveled back to Jerusalem asking everyone they saw, "Have you seen a boy named Jesus?"

Finally, they went into God's house in Jerusalem. There was Jesus! Jesus was sitting among the teachers and leaders of God's house.

"We were worried about you," Mary said.

Jesus answered, "Didn't you know I had to be in my Father's house?"

You come to God's house to learn about God, too. Jesus loved God's house, just like you!

~Based on Luke 2:41-51

 ## Story Review

1. Where did Mary and Joseph take Jesus? Mary and Joseph took Jesus to God's house.

2. Where was Jesus when Mary and Joseph couldn't find Him? Jesus was in God's house.

3. What did Jesus say to Mary? Jesus said, "Didn't you know I had to be in my Father's house?"

 ## Parent Corner

1. *Feeding time sharing.* At feeding time show your baby the story poster. Tell the story while your baby looks at the poster. Ask and answer the discussion questions on the page. Repeat the story, memory verse or lesson theme several times while feeding your child.

2. When you take the baby to church say, **Jesus loved God's house, just like you.**

3. Use building blocks to play together. Pretend to build a church. Say, **This is God's house. We love to go to God's house. Our memory verse says, "Let us go to the house of the Lord."**

Bulletin Board

What You Need

- pattern on page 21
- clear adhesive-backed plastic
- card stock
- craft foam (optional)

What To Do

1. Depending on how you want to use the poster (see ideas below), enlarge, reduce or simply copy page 21 to fit your bulletin board space.
2. To make a take-home paper, duplicate the story page to the back of story poster.
3. To use the poster as an in-class activity, duplicate the pattern to card stock (or craft foam). Cut the page into two or three simple puzzle pieces. Help the children assemble the puzzle.

Story Poster

⊪⇒ Poster Pointer

Use a thumb tack to fasten a plastic page protector pocket onto the wall just outside your nursery room door. Each week, slip the story poster inside the pocket so parents will see what their child is learning in church.

God's House

Let us go to the house of the Lord.

~Psalm 122:1

Read to Me

. . . .

what you Need
- pages 22 and 23 duplicated
- construction paper
- scissors
- glue
- tape

what To Do

1. Before class, cut out the church pattern. Use the pattern to trace 5 church shapes onto construction paper. Cut out the 5 church shapes. Glue the church pattern to one of the construction paper shapes. Cut out the 4 squares from page 23. Glue each square onto a church shape. You will have a total of 5 church-shaped pages.
2. Lay all 5 pages out on a table. Tape the seams together so the pages will fold accordion style into a book.
3. Let the children hold the book. Read the phrases while you help them unfold the book into a long story page.

God's House

INSide God's House Folding Picture Book

Jesus loved God's house, just like ME!

Coloring

What You Need
- duplicated page
- crayons

What To Do
1. Show the baby the picture of the church. Say, **This is God's house. Jesus loved God's house, just like you.**
2. Help older babies scribble-color the picture.

House of the Lord Coloring Page

God's House

I Love God's House

What You Need
- duplicated page

What To Do
1. Say the rhyme. Try to get some of the older babies to say the rhyme with you.
2. Do the actions, helping the children do them with you.

I

[point to self]

love

[touch heart]

God's

[point upward to God]

house

[form roof over head with hands]

God's House

25

Stained Glass Church Windows

What You Need

- duplicated page for each child
- transparency sheets
- permanent markers
- scissors
- tape
- crayons
- yarn

What To Do

1. Before class, cut out the church.
2. Cut two pieces of transparency a little bigger than the windows. Trace the stained glass pattern on each transparency piece. Color with multiple colors of permanent markers.
3. Cut out windows from the pattern pages.
4. Tape the transparency windows behind the cut-out windows of picture.
5. Tape a loop of yarn at the top of the picture for a hanger.
6. Say, **What pretty windows we have put in our church!**

26

House of the Lord Collage

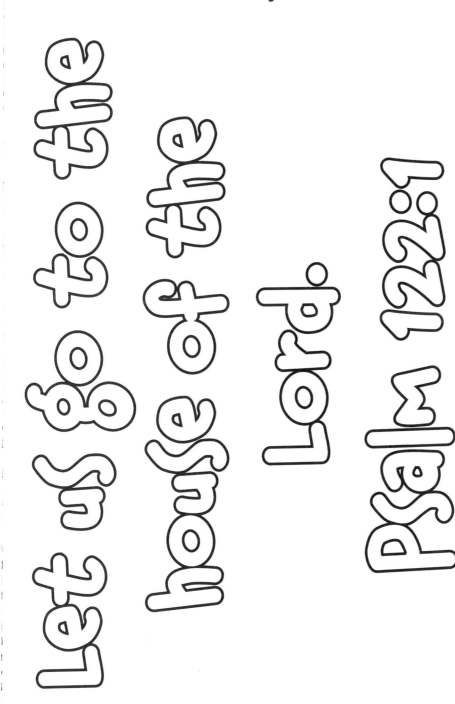

Let us go to the house of the Lord. Psalm 122:1

Optional
Fill in the letters of the verse with glitter, markers, colored cereals, small sticker dots or other interesting items.

Bulletin Board

What You Need
- duplicated page
- construction paper
- magazine pictures of various church buildings
- stapler
- markers or glitter and glue (optional)

What To Do
1. Before class, mount several magazine pictures of church buildings onto brightly colored construction paper pieces. Cut out the verse picture from the pattern page and attach it to the top center of a bulletin board. Attach the church pictures to the bulletin board.
2. During class, let the children touch the pictures. Say, **Some churches look the same, and some look different from others. They are all God's house. Jesus loved God's house just like you.**

God's House

Room Decoration

what you Need

- duplicated page for each welcome sign
- shoebox lid for each welcome sign
- foil or wrapping paper
- scissors
- glue
- thumb tack to hang

what To Do

1. Before class, cover the inside and/or outside of a shoebox lid with foil or wrapping paper. Cut the welcome sign from the pattern page. Glue the welcome sign in the center inside of the shoebox lid.
2. Hang a welcome sign on your nursery room door.
3. You might want to have older babies scribble-color some of the pattern page signs and make several welcome signs to put around the church building. Write on the signs, "From the Nursery Department."

Welcome Sign

what To Do, continued...

4. Show the babies the sign on your door. Say, **We have a sign to tell people "Welcome to God's house." Jesus loved God's house, just like you.**

God's House

Chapter 3

Jesus Had Friends, Just Like Me

Memory Verse

"Come follow me," Jesus said.

~Matthew 4:19

 Story to Share

Jesus needed some helpers so He could go all over and do good work for God. Peter and Andrew were fishing in the sea. "Come follow me," Jesus said. Peter and Andrew left their fishing nets and followed Jesus to be His friends.

Later, Jesus saw James and John. "Come," Jesus said. James and John left their fishing boats and followed Jesus, too.

Peter, Andrew, James and John were Jesus' special friends. Jesus found some other friends to help Him, too.

Jesus had friends, just like you.

~Based on Matthew 4:18-22

 Story Review

1. What did Jesus say to Peter and Andrew? Jesus said, "Come, follow me."

2. What did Peter, Andrew, James and John do when Jesus called them? They followed Jesus and became His friends.

Parent Corner

1. *Together coloring time.* Sit at a table and hold your baby. Place the story poster on the table. Help your baby hold a crayon and scribble-color the story poster. Tell the story while the baby is coloring.

2. Play follow the leader with your child. Non-crawling babies can mimic your actions such as waving arms, making a funny face, etc. Say, **Follow me. That's what Jesus said. Jesus had friends just like you do.**

3. Take a snapshot of your child's nursery class. Post the picture on the refrigerator at home. Say often, **Here is Jacob. This is Angela. They are your friends. You have friends just like Jesus did.**

Bulletin Board

. . . .

What You Need

- pattern on page 31
- clear adhesive-backed plastic
- produce bag net (onion, potatoes, etc.)

What To Do

1. Depending on how you want to use the poster (see ideas below), enlarge, reduce or simply copy page 31 to fit your bulletin board space.
2. To make a take-home paper, duplicate the story page to the back of story poster.
3. To use the poster as an in-class activity, cut a piece of produce net bag for each child to glue onto the poster.

Friends

∾⊕⊙ Story Poster ⊙⊕∾

▭═▷ Poster Pointer

Reduce size of poster picture to about one-half. Cover both sides of poster with clear adhesive-backed plastic. Use scissors to round off sharp corners. Let each child hold a covered story poster while you tell the story.

"Come follow me," Jesus said.

~Matthew 4:19

Hands On

what you Need

- duplicated page
- empty bank check box
- glue
- 4 wrapped, flat lollipops
- marker

what To Do

1. Before class, cut the rectangle from the pattern page. Glue the rectangle to the top of the check box. Poke the four marked holes. Draw a smiling face on each of the lollipops.
2. Let the children handle the lollipop puppets. Help them put the four puppets in the holes in the scene. Say, **Jesus called Peter and Andrew away from their fishing nets. Jesus called James and John away from their fishing boat. They all followed Jesus and became His friends. Jesus had friends just like you do.**

Friends

Lollipop Puppets

finished craft

Come Follow Me

Follow me and be my friend

Be my friend

Be my friend

Follow and be my friend

Jesus said, "Follow me."

(Repeat song and insert child's name.)

Follow me, Allie, and be my friend

Be my friend

Be my friend...

what you Need
- duplicated page
- crayons

what To Do
1. Sing the song, "Come, Follow Me" to the tune of "London Bridge."
2. Repeat the song, inserting a child's name after "follow me."
3. Older babies will enjoy coloring the poster to take home.

Friends

Easy Craft

What You Need

- duplicated page
- oval or oblong ice cream carton lids, about 5 x 7 inches
- purchased quick-dry dough or craft clay

What To Do

1. Before class, let parents know what you plan to do, so they may give permission, as this will be a nice keepsake for them. Some may volunteer to help with this project. Cut the verse strip from the page and glue it to the side of the ice cream lids.

2. Place some dough inside the lid and flatten it as much as possible.

3. Press baby's footprint (or both footprints) into the clay or dough.

4. Wash baby's feet and set the craft aside.

Footprints Plaque

"Come follow me," Jesus said. Matthew 4:19

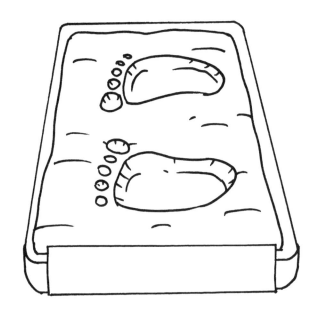

What To Do, continued...

5. Before the clay or dough dries use a pencil or toothpick to scratch baby's first name and the date of the footprints.

6. Say to baby, **Jesus said, "Come follow me."**

Friends Make Me Happy Picture

Puzzle

What You Need
- duplicated page
- crayons

What To Do
1. Help the children finish the picture by adding a smile to each "friend's" face.
2. Say, **Jesus was happy to make new friends. We are happy to have friends, too.**
3. Jesus had friends, just like me.

Friends

Learning Play

what you Need

- duplicated page
- instant oatmeal or toaster pastry box
- scissors
- animal cookies or similar
- glue or tape

what To Do

1. Before class, cut the two labels from the pattern page. Glue or tape a label to the front and the back of the box.

2. Cut a shape from the front, back, and each side of the box. Cutouts should be large enough for an animal cookie to fit through.

3. Show the children how to put cookies through the holes. Say, **Emily put a friend in the triangle. Where is Emily's friend? He is hiding in the box. There is Emily's friend. Jesus had friends, just like Emily.**

Friends

Hide and Seek Friends

Hide and Seek Friends Game.

Jesus had friends, just like me.

finished craft

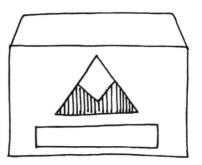

what To Do, continued...

4. Open the top of the box to find the cookies the child has put inside. Use a different set of cookies for each child, in case a child puts cookies in his/her mouth.

Chapter 4

Jesus Loved God's Word, Just Like Me

Memory Verse

Blessed... are those who hear the Word of God.

~Luke 11:28

 ## Story to Share

Jesus was getting ready to go teach people about God. First Jesus was baptized. Then the devil tried to get Jesus to do some things that were wrong, just like the devil tries to get us to do things that are wrong.

But Jesus knew all of God's Word. He answered the devil three times with God's Holy Word. Then the devil left and God's angels took care of Jesus.

Jesus loved God's Word, just like you. Isn't it fun to sit and listen to stories from God's Word? That is how we can keep from doing wrong things. We can learn God's Word and give an answer to everyone who tries to get us to do wrong.

~Based on Matthew 4:1-11

 ## Story Review

1. Who tried to get Jesus to do some wrong things? The devil tried to get Jesus to do some wrong things.

2. How did Jesus answer the devil? Jesus answered the devil with God's Word.

3. How can we answer someone who is trying to get us to do something wrong? We can answer with God's Word.

 ## Parent Corner

1. Make use of waiting time. When you are waiting in a doctor's office, a lobby or even a long line at the super market, tell the story to your baby. This will help keep your baby from becoming restless and fussy and will reinforce the Bible truth once again.

2. Open your Bible and read the story directly from the Bible. Instill in your child the difference between cartoon stories and God's true Word.

3. Purchase a children's Bible suitable to your child's age. Use it often to read to your baby.

Bulletin Board

what you Need

- pattern on page 39
- clear adhesive-backed plastic
- black construction paper
- glue

what To Do

1. Depending on how you want to use the poster (see ideas below), enlarge, reduce, or simply copy page 39 to fit your bulletin board space.
2. To make a take-home paper, duplicate the story page to the back of story poster.
3. To use the poster as an in-class activity, let the children glue strips of black construction paper around the edges of the Bible cover.

⤳ Story Poster ⤳

▭▻ Poster Pointer

Attach the poster to brightly colored paper. Fasten the poster to the bulletin board. Carry children to the bulletin board several times during class time. Say the memory verse or retell the story while you help the child touch the story poster.

God's word

Blessed... are those who hear the Word of God.

~Luke 11:28

Bible BookMark

Easy Craft

What You Need
- duplicated page
- tape
- crayons

What To Do
1. Before class, cut the bookmark from the pattern page.
2. Help children fold the bookmarks in half. Tape the seams.
3. Older children will enjoy coloring the bookmark.
4. Place a sample bookmark in your Bible to show children what they are for. Send a bookmark home with each child.
5. If you have extra time, have the children help make bookmarks to give to members of another class.

BIBLE

"Blessed are those who hear the word of God."
~Luke 11:28

God's Word

My Bible Song

🎵 🎵

🎵

Song

. . . .

what you Need
• duplicated page

what To Do
1. Sing the song, "My Bible," to the tune of "Jesus Loves Me."
2. Let the children hold a Bible or the story poster while you help them sing the song again.

My Bible

My Bible is God's Word.
My Bible tells about my Lord.
It has great stories, yes indeed.
Won't you read my Bible to me?

[chorus]
Listen to God's Word,
Listen to God's Word,
Listen to God's Word,
My Bible is God's Word.

God's word

Rhyme

What You Need
• duplicated page

What To Do
1. Say the rhyme, using the simple actions.
2. Help children do the actions with you.

 # God's Word Action Rhyme

Jesus loved God's word.
[point to God]

He knew it by heart.
[put hands on heart]

I love God's word, too.
[make praying hands]

I'll keep it in my own heart.
[point at self]

God's word

I Love God's Word Coloring Book

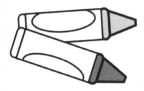

Coloring

what you Need
- pages 43 and 44, duplicated
- stapler
- crayons (two or three in a bag to take home with coloring book)

what To Do
1. Before class, cut out pages.
2. Staple pages together so they form a book.
3. Let children scribble-color the page while you say, **I love reading God's Word with my teacher. I love reading God's Word at church. I love God's Word all the time!**
4. Send the coloring book home with children.

I Love God's Word

BIBLE

God's word

I love reading God's Word at church and with my family.

I love reading God's Word with my teachers before my nap.

Hidden Pictures Puzzle

Puzzle

what you Need
- duplicated page
- crayons

what To Do
1. Discuss the picture with the children. Say, **The little boy and girl are reading God's Word at Sunday school class. Jesus loved God's Word, too, just like you.**
2. Help the children find 3 hidden Bibles in the picture.

God's word

৵৹ Chapter 5 ৵৹

Jesus Liked to Help, Just Like Me

Memory Verse

He thanked [Jesus].
~Luke 17:16

 ## Story to Share

Jesus was traveling to a village to tell people about God. Suddenly, ten men called to Him. They were sick with leprosy.

"Jesus!" they called. "Please help us and make us well."

Jesus said, "You will be well. Go and show yourselves to the priest."

The men went away quickly. But one man saw that he was already well. He turned and came back. "Thank you, Jesus!" he said. "Thank you."

Jesus was happy to make the man well. Jesus liked to help people. You can help people, too. There are many ways we can help people.
~Based on Luke 17:11-19

 ## Story Review

1. How many men asked Jesus to make them well? Ten men asked Jesus to make them well.

2. How many men came back to thank Jesus? Only one man came back to thank Jesus.

3. Who else can help people? We can help people in many ways.

 ## Parent Corner

1. *Bedtime storytelling.* Pat your baby's arm or shoulder while telling the Bible story in a soothing voice. Retell the story until your baby falls asleep.

2. Let your baby sit on your lap while you are doing chores. Say, **What a good helper you are. Thank you for helping me.**

3. Take notice when someone in the household does something helpful. Say, **Brother is doing a wonderful job helping pick up toys. Thank you, Brother.**

Bulletin Board

What You Need

- pattern on page 49
- clear adhesive-backed plastic
- bandage strips

What To Do

1. Depending on how you want to use the poster (see ideas below), enlarge, reduce or simply copy page 49 to fit your bulletin board space.
2. To make a take-home paper, duplicate the story page to the back of story poster.
3. To use the poster as an in-class activity, help the children stick bandage strips around the edge of the poster to form a frame. Say, **Jesus helped the men be well.**

Jesus Helped

☙ Story Poster ☙

▭▭▷ Poster Pointer

Reduce the size of the poster to fit the sides of plastic baby wipe containers. Glue or securely tape one poster picture to at least one side of each container. Make at least three or four blocks, or make one block with poster pictures from each of the eight stories in this book. Help the children stack the blocks. Point to the poster picture for the current lesson and retell the story or say the memory verse with the children.

He thanked [Jesus].

~Luke 17:16

Puzzle

What You Need

• duplicated page
• crayons
•

What To Do

1. Help the children match the boys and girls who are working to the tools they need to complete their helping task.
2. For younger babies, you may want to simply hold their hand and trace the lines while you discuss the helping tasks.
3. For older babies, help them trace the lines from the tools to the children.

Jesus Helped

What Helpers Use

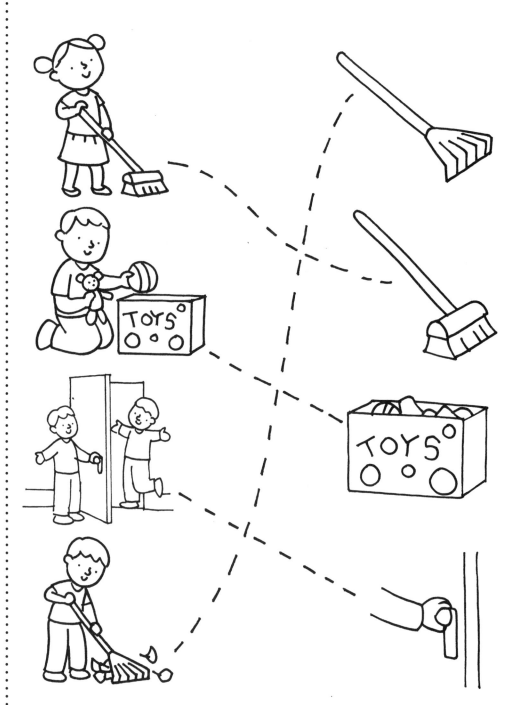

Jesus liked to help others, just like me.

Jesus Helped

Jesus helped
ten men,

He made them
well again,

But only one came
back to say:

Thanks for helping me!

Song

. . . .

what you Need
• duplicated page

what To Do
1. Sing the song "Jesus Helped" to the tune of "Row, Row, Row Your Boat."
2. Sing the song again, helping children make praying hands on the last line.

51

Jesus Helped

Learning Play

What You Need

- duplicated pages 52 and 53 (two pages)
- beach ball
- tape
- scissors

What To Do

1. Before class, cut out the four scenes from the two pattern pages. Tape the four scenes around the ball.
2. Roll the ball to the children. Let each baby handle the ball. Point to a picture and discuss it.
3. Say, **Jesus helped ten men who were sick. One man came back to say, "Thank you." A boy is helping his mom fold towels. Mommy is giving a thank-you hug. Jesus liked to help others, just like you.**

Story Ball

Jesus Helped

finished craft

Read to Me

What You Need

- pages 54, 55 and 56 duplicated to card stock
- scissors
- hole punch
- plastic rings

What To Do

1. Before class, cut out the hand pages and slip them between two sheets of construction paper. Glue the book cover to the front piece of construction paper.
2. Punch 3 holes through all layers of the book at the left edge. Fasten three plastic rings through the holes to hold the book together.
3. Hold each baby on your lap. Turn the pages as you read the book to the children. Babies love repetition and the soothing sound of your voice. This is a good one-on-one activity for teachers and children.

* Hand-Shape Book *

Daddy Gets Some Help

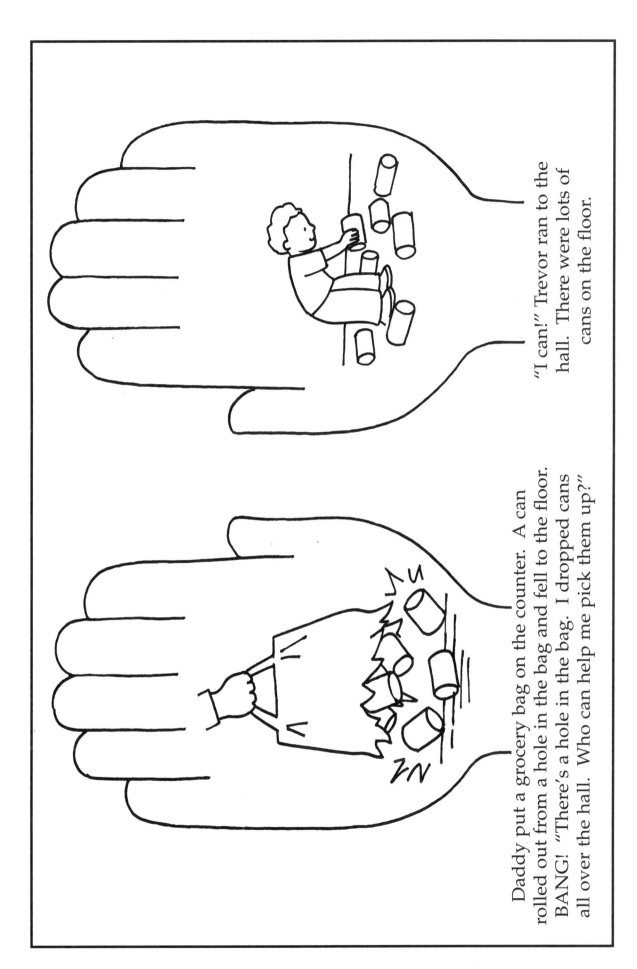

Daddy put a grocery bag on the counter. A can rolled out from a hole in the bag and fell to the floor. BANG! "There's a hole in the bag. I dropped cans all over the hall. Who can help me pick them up?"

"I can!" Trevor ran to the hall. There were lots of cans on the floor.

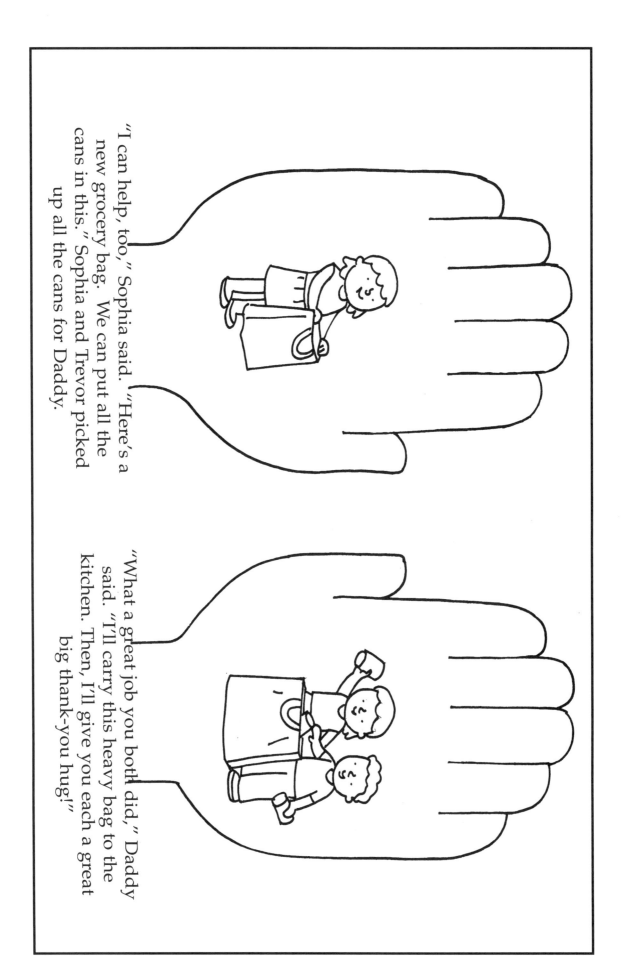

"I can help, too," Sophia said. "Here's a new grocery bag. We can put all the cans in this." Sophia and Trevor picked up all the cans for Daddy.

"What a great job you both did," Daddy said. "I'll carry this heavy bag to the kitchen. Then, I'll give you each a great big thank-you hug!"

Chapter 6

Jesus Loves Others, Just Like Me

Memory Verse

Love one another.

~John 13:34

Story to Share

Jesus and His friends were gathered together, just like your family gets together, to eat dinner. But before the meal was served, Jesus did something His friends thought was very odd. Jesus bent down and began to wash the feet of His friends.

"What are you doing?" Peter asked. "You are our Lord. Why are you washing our feet?"

Jesus answered, "I am being an example. I am showing you how to show love to others. You can do many things to show love to others."

Jesus loved others and wanted to show us how to love others, too. We don't usually wash each others' smelly feet, do we? But Jesus wanted us to know that we should do anything we can to show love to others.

Jesus loved others, and still loves them! Just like you.

~Based on John 13:1-17

Story Review

1. What did Jesus do for His friends? Jesus washed His friends' feet.

2. Why did Jesus wash His friends' feet? Jesus wanted to show us that we should do anything we can to show love to others.

Parent Corner

1. *In the car.* Tell the Bible story while riding in the car. Say or sing the memory verse or story theme in a fun way. Any tune will be entertaining for the baby.

2. While you're changing your baby's diaper, it is a great time to discuss how important it is that we do things for others.

3. Help your baby show love for someone by placing cookies in a bag and allowing your baby to give them to someone you know.

Bulletin Board

what You Need
- pattern on page 59
- clear adhesive-backed plastic
- felt or fabric scraps

what To Do
1. Depending on how you want to use the poster (see ideas below and at left), enlarge, reduce or simply copy page 59 to fit your bulletin board space.
2. To use the poster as an in-class activity, glue a felt or fabric scrap to Jesus' waist, long enough that he could use it to dry Peter's feet. Also, you may want to let the children add some heart stickers to the poster to indicate loving one another.

Loves

⤳ Story Poster ⤳

▦⟶ Poster Pointer

Make easy take-home bags by taping a story poster to a paper grocery bag for each child. Be sure to write the child's name on the bag.

Love one another.

~John 13:34

Room Decoration

What You Need

- page duplicated to transparency sheets
- scissors
- fishing line
- tape
- red permanent markers

What To Do

1. Before class, cut the hearts from the transparency sheets. Tape a length of fishing line to each heart. Hang the hearts in windows or close to a light fixture.
2. Let the babies see and touch the sun catchers. Say, **Jesus loved others, just like you.**

Love Others Sun Catchers

LOVE ONE ANOTHER
John 13:34

Loves

Love One Another Song

Song

what you Need
- duplicated page

what To Do
1. Sing the song to the tune of "Wheels on the Bus."
2. Encourage older babies to sing the song with you.
3. Add an action by touching your heart every time you say the word "love."

Jesus said to love one another,

love one another,

love one another,

Jesus said to love one another.

Love everyone.

Loves

Hands On

. . . .

What You Need

- duplicated page
- felt
- cotton for stuffing
- glue

What To Do

1. Before class, use the pattern on the page to cut out two hearts from felt for each child.
2. Cut a ½ x 6 inch strip of felt for a handle.
3. Glue the two hearts together, leaving a small space to stuff the heart.
4. Glue the handle to the top of the heart. Stuff cotton inside the heart. Glue the remainder of the edge closed.
5. Let babies play with the hearts. Say, **God wants us to love one another. Jesus loved others just like you.**

❧ Soft Heart Rattles ❧

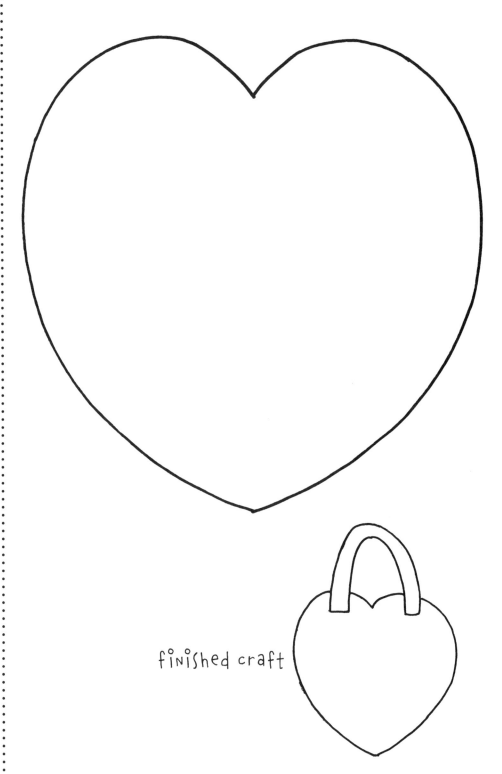

finished craft

Love One Another Puzzle

Puzzle

What You Need
- duplicated page
- crayons

What To Do

1. Help the children hold a crayon and trace the lines from the child to someone he/she can show love to. Say, **Let's trace this line and see who we can show love to. It's Grandpa! We can show love to Grandpa. Now let's try another line.**
2. Older babies may enjoy coloring the pictures. With younger babies, you may want to hold their hand and help them trace the line without using a crayon.
3. The children will enjoy the active play and the conversation with you as teacher.

Loves

Rhyme

. . . .

What You Need
• duplicated page

What To Do
1. Do the actions while you say the rhyme with the children.
2. Get the children involved in doing the actions. Make it as fun as you can, either in a one-on-one situation or with a group of little children.

Loves

❧ Show My Love ❧ Action Rhyme

I show my love
by giving a hug.
[hug self or another child]
I love you.

I show my love
by helping a friend.
*[clasp hands together
or hold hands with a friend]*
I love you.

I show my love
by praying for you.
[bow heads in prayer]
I love you.

Heart Bubble Wands

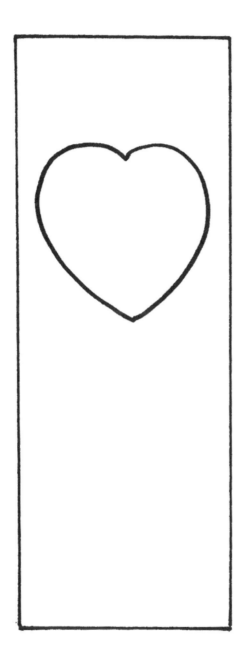

Recipe for Bubble Solution

Mix ½ cup liquid dish detergent with ½ cup water. Add soap to the water, rather than water to the soap to avoid excessively foamy suds. Stir gently. Store in plastic container with lid until ready to use.

Learning Play

What You Need
- duplicated page
- plastic milk jug
- scissors
- liquid dish detergent
- water
- plastic container

What To Do
1. Cut the wand pattern from the page. Trace the pattern onto the side of a plastic milk jug. Cut the wand from the jug. Mix the bubble solution in a plastic container.
2. Make some bubbles for children to see. Say, **The bubbles look like hearts. Hearts mean love. We show our love for others. Jesus loved others, just like you.**
3. Older babies may enjoy trying to make some bubbles.

Loves

I Love You Handprint

Easy Craft

what you Need
• duplicated page
• yarn
• tape
• washable paint
• shallow pan
• cleanup cloths

what To Do
1. Attach a loop of yarn to the top of the heart for a hanger.
2. Spread some washable paint in a shallow pan.
3. Dip each baby's hand into the paint, then press it onto the picture.

I LOVE YOU!

Loves

Chapter 7

Jesus Told Others About God, Just Like Me

Memory Verse

Mary sat listening to what [Jesus] said.
~Luke 10:39

Story to Share

Jesus went to visit his good friends Mary and Martha. Martha hurried around the house to make everything just right. Things must be clean for their friend Jesus. A nice supper must be prepared for their friend Jesus. There was much to do.

But Mary sat at the feet of Jesus and listened to Him talk about God. Mary loved to hear about God.

Martha became angry and wanted Mary to help with the work. But Jesus said, "What Mary is doing the right thing. She is listening to hear about God."

Jesus told others about God, just like you! You can tell others about God. You can invite someone to come to church and hear about God. You can share a story poster from Sunday school. You can give a Bible to someone who doesn't have one.

~Based on Luke 10:38-42

Story Review

1. Who were Jesus' friends? Mary and Martha were Jesus' friends.

2. Why was Martha angry? Martha wanted Mary to help with all the work instead of listening to Jesus tell about God.

3. What did Jesus say to Martha? Jesus told Martha that Mary was doing the right thing.

Parent Corner

1. Invite some of the other nursery families to your home for a snack and Bible story time. Say to the babies, **We can tell others about God. Jesus told others about God, just like we can.**

Bulletin Board

What You Need
- pattern on page 69
- clear adhesive-backed plastic

What To Do
1. Depending on how you want to use the poster (see ideas below), enlarge, reduce or simply copy page 69 to fit your bulletin board space.
2. To make a take-home paper, duplicate the story page to the back of story poster.
3. To use the poster as an in-class activity, cut the rectangle from this page. Help children glue the image in the marked rectangle on the poster.

Told Others

Story Poster

▭▭▷ Poster Pointer

To make a storybook, copy the poster for each lesson in this book to card stock. You may laminate the pages with clear self-adhesive, if you wish. Place the eight posters together. Punch the left edge with a three-ring hole punch. Fasten the book together with plastic rings in the three holes on the left edge. Use the book as a read-to-me activity for rocking-chair time or playtime.

Mary sat listening to what [Jesus] said.

~Luke 10:39

Song

what you Need
• duplicated page

what To Do
1. Sing the song "Telling Friends About God" to the tune of "Mary Had a Little Lamb."

Telling Friends About God

Jesus told his friends about God

Friends about God

Friends about God

Jesus told his friends about God

Jesus told his friends, just like me.

I can tell my friends about God

Friends about God

Friends about God

I can tell my friends about God

Jesus told his friends, just like me.

Told Others

Hear about God, Action Rhyme

Rhyme

what you Need
• duplicated page

what To Do
1. Say the rhyme, using the actions.
2. Help children do the actions while you say the rhyme again.

Mary listened to Jesus.

[touch ear]

Martha worked
really hard.

Jesus said, "Martha,
come listen."

[touch ear]

It's important to
hear about God.

[point to God]

Sometimes we're
working so hard,
we forget to listen.

[touch ear]

Jesus wants us
to remember,

[point to forehead]

It's important to hear
about God.

[point to God]

Told Others

71

Read to Me

What You Need

- duplicated pages 72, 73 and 74 for each book
- five pieces of construction paper for each book
- scissors
- glue
- staples

What To Do

1. Before class, cut the two cover pages from page 72. Cut the two other pages into the four marked sections. Staple five pieces of construction paper together.
2. Glue the sections marked A onto the five stapled pages, beginning with the book cover section. Next, flip the book upside down, so that the staples remain on the left hand side. Glue the sections marked B onto the five empty pages.
3. Read the story about Jesus and His friends, Mary and Martha, to the child.

Told Others

Double Story Book

Jesus Told Others About God

cover page A

I Can Tell Others About God

cover page B

What To Do, continued...

4. Flip the book over and read the "I Can..." book to the child.

Mary sat and listened to Jesus talk about God.

Martha was busy getting a meal ready to eat and cleaning house.

"Jesus," Martha said, "tell my sister to help me do all this work."

"Martha, my friend," Jesus said, "Mary is doing the right thing. You, too, need to sit and listen about God."

I can invite someone
to church.

I can share my Sunday school
paper with someone.

I can tell someone
God loves them.

I can tell others
I pray for them.

Telling About God Phone

Hands On

What You Need
- duplicated page
- scissors
- craft foam or cardboard
- yarn
- tape

What To Do
1. Before class, use the patterns on the duplicated page to trace and cut out the telephone.
2. Let the children handle the telephone. Say, **Oh, who are you talking to? Kyle is telling someone about God. Oh, listen to Mia tell her friend about God.**

Told Others

Easy Craft

What You Need

- duplicated page for each child
- crayons

What To Do

1. Help the children color their pictures.
2. Take the pictures to another class. Let older babies hand a picture to someone in the other class.
3. Say, **We are using our pretty pictures to tell others about God. Jesus told his friends about God, just like me.**

☙ Tell Others ❧
Coloring Picture to Share

Chapter 8

Jesus Prayed to God, Just Like Me

Memory Verse

Watch and pray.
~Mark 14:38

 **Story to Share**

It was almost time for Jesus to do something very important. Jesus was going to die on a cross for us. Jesus wanted to talk to God. He took His friends with Him and went away from all the many people who followed to listen to Him teach and to be healed by Him.

Jesus knelt down and prayed to God.

After a while, Jesus went to find His friends. They were sleeping. He tried to wake them, then left again.

Jesus prayed again to God.

Jesus prayed to God, just like you. Isn't it wonderful to know we can talk to God anytime?

~Based on Mark 14:32-39

 **Story Review**

1. Who did Jesus want to talk to? Jesus wanted to talk to God.

2. Who can we talk to anytime we want? We can pray to God anytime we want.

 Parent Corner

1. *Read-to-me time.* Hold your baby on your lap while sitting in your favorite story time chair. Open your Bible or picture Bible to the Scripture listed above. Let your baby touch the Bible or picture Bible to help instill in your child that you are telling a truthful story from God's Word.

2. Pray at different times during the day with your child. Instill the concept that we don't have to recite memorized prayers at mealtime or bedtime, and that we may talk to God anytime we want.

Bulletin Board

What You Need
- pattern on page 79
- clear adhesive-backed plastic
- praying hands stickers

What To Do
1. Depending on how you want to use the poster (see ideas below), enlarge, reduce or simply copy page 79 to fit your bulletin board space.
2. To make a take-home paper, duplicate the story page to the back of the story poster.
3. To use the poster as an in-class activity, help children place some praying hands stickers on the poster.

Prayed

๛๏ Story Poster ๏๛

▬▬▷ Poster Pointer

Have children take turns placing a sticker or sticker dot on the poster. Laminate a few of the posters on brightly colored paper and trim the corners to remove any sharp edges, then let each child put a sticker on the border of the poster. Simply take turns putting stickers on until each child has had at least one turn.

watch and pray.

~mark 14:38

♪ ♪ ♪
Song

what you Need
- duplicated page
- thinned watercolor paints
- cotton swabs

what To Do
1. Sing the song to the tune of "The Bear Went Over the Mountain."
2. Older children will enjoy painting the poster with thinned watercolor paints using the cotton swabs.
3. Send the poster home with each baby so parents can sing the song with them, too.

Prayed

✎ Praying Song Poster ✎

Jesus loved to pray to God

Jesus loved to pray to God

Jesus loved to pray to God

I love to pray to God, too.

Jesus prayed just like me

Jesus prayed just like me

Jesus prayed just like me

God loves to hear from me.

Prayer Plaque

Easy Craft

What You Need
- duplicated page
- crayons
- miniature marshmallows
- glue
- yarn
- tape
-

What To Do
1. Before class, tape a loop of yarn to the top of the plaque for a hanger.
2. Let older children color the pictures on the plaque.
3. Help children glue mini marshmallows around the edge of the plaque for a frame.
4. Say, **See Jesus praying to God? See the girl praying to God? Jesus prayed to God just like you.**

Prayed

Learning Play

What You Need

- this page duplicated for each child
- pages 83 and 84 duplicated to card stock for each child
- paper lunch bag for each child
- scissors
- tape or glue

What To Do

1. Before class, cut the label from the instruction page.
2. Glue or tape the label to a paper lunch bag for each child. Cut the four prayer cards from card stock. Round the corners so they will not be sharp.
3. Place the cards inside the bag for each child. Let the children take the cards from the bag and put them back as they wish.
4. Say, **Here is a picture of a sick friend. You can pray for a sick friend.** Repeat for each picture card.

Prayed

I CAN PRAY

I can pray for my mom and dad.

I can pray for a sick friend.

I can pray for my
Nursery friends.

I can pray for
my pastor.

Chapter 9

More Just Like Me Activities

Just Like Me Song

Sing the song "Just Like Me" to the tune of "London Bridge."

Jesus did good just like me
Just like me
Just like me
Jesus did good just like me
Just like me!

Jesus and I work for God
Work for God
Work for God
Jesus and I work for God
Jesus and I.

God is very proud of me
Proud of me
Proud of me
God is very proud of me
God loves us all!

Easy Craft

What You Need

- pages 86 and 87 duplicated, enough copies to fit around bulletin board
- crayons or markers
- tape

What To Do

1. Cut the border strips on solid lines. Tape together to make long border strips. Color the pictures as you wish with crayons or markers.
2. Use the border for a bulletin board with magazine pictures of children or photos of the children in your nursery class.
3. Use the text on the instruction page as the bulletin board heading.

More

Bulletin Board Border

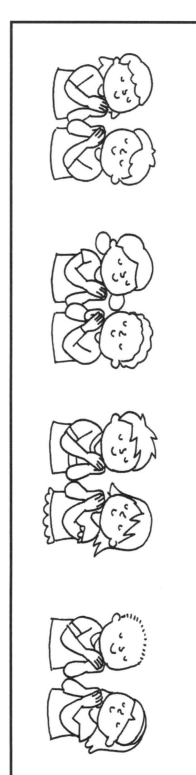

JESUS DID GOOD THINGS FOR GOD, JUST LIKE ME.

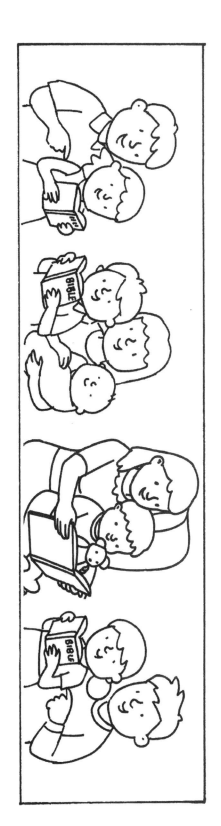

Puzzle

what you Need

- page 89 or 90 duplicated to the back of a story poster
- scissors
- envelope to hold puzzle pieces
- optional craft foam or cardboard

what To Do

1. Choose the difficulty level of the two puzzle patterns. Duplicate the one you want to use to the back of a story poster. You may choose to duplicate the puzzle and poster onto card stock for easier handling by children.
2. You may also want to make a thicker puzzle for small hands. Just duplicate both the puzzle page and story poster to card stock. Glue a sheet of craft foam or cardboard between the two pages. Let the glue dry, then cut out the puzzle pieces.
3. You may want to make a puzzle from each lesson's story poster, to use for playtime or one-on-one time.

More

Easy Puzzle

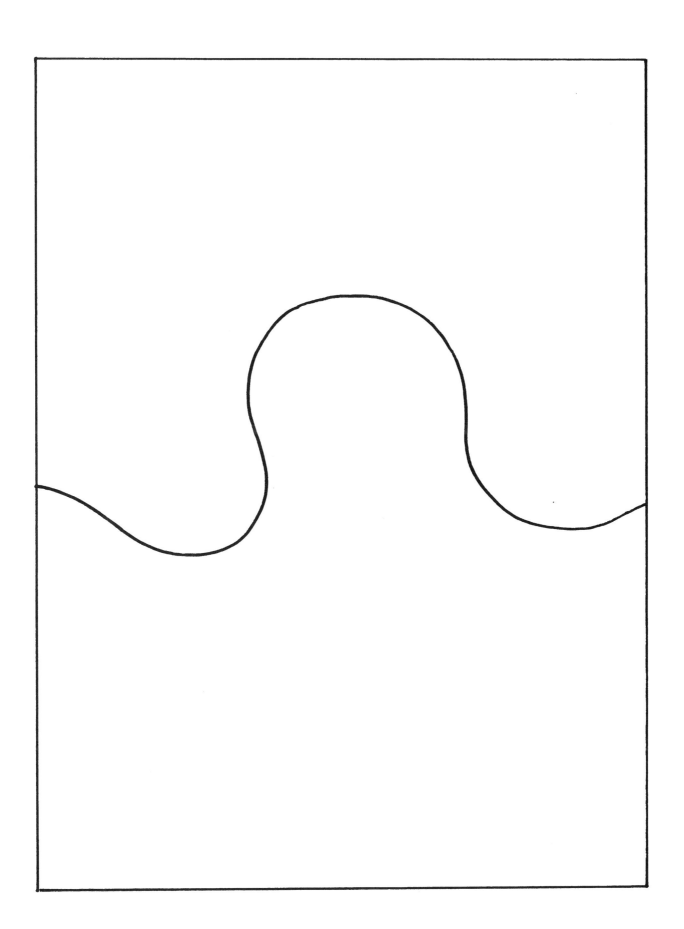

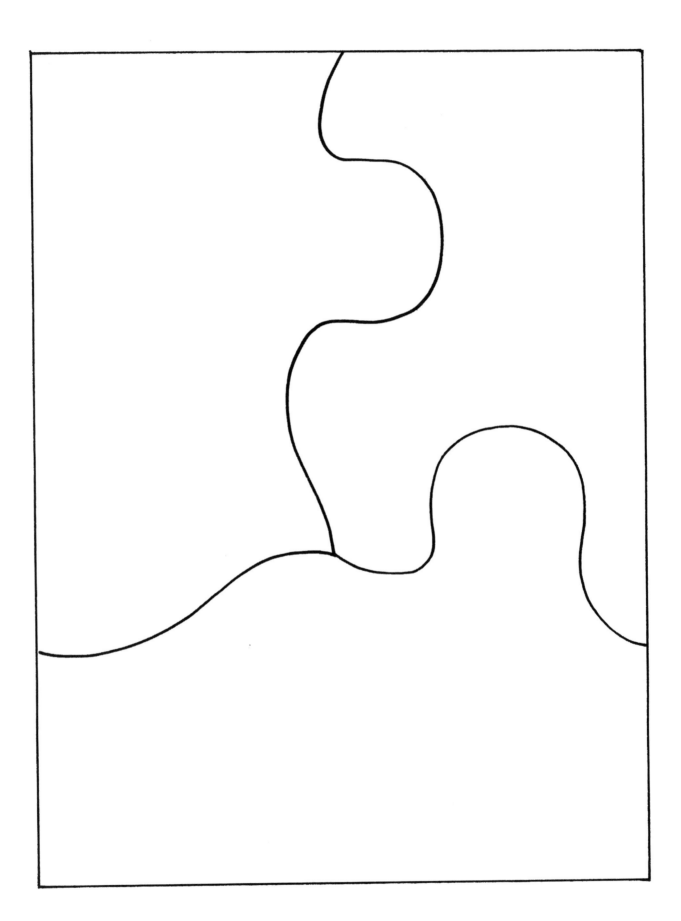

Just Like Me Picture Book

Just Like Me

What You Need

- pages 91-95, duplicated to card stock for each child (5 pages total)
- instant camera or photo from home of each child
- hole punch
- plastic rings

What To Do

1. Before class, cut apart the pages as marked to make 9 pages total. Put the pages in order and punch holes along the left side of the book.
2. Glue each baby's picture on the back page of the book.
3. Read the book to each baby. Say often, **Just like me**.

More

Jesus was a baby, just like me.

Jesus loved God's house, just like me.

Jesus had friends, just like me.

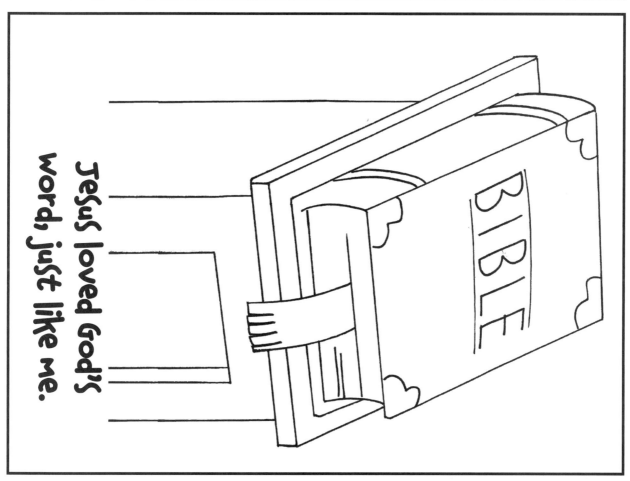

Jesus loved God's word, just like me.

Jesus liked to help,
just like me.

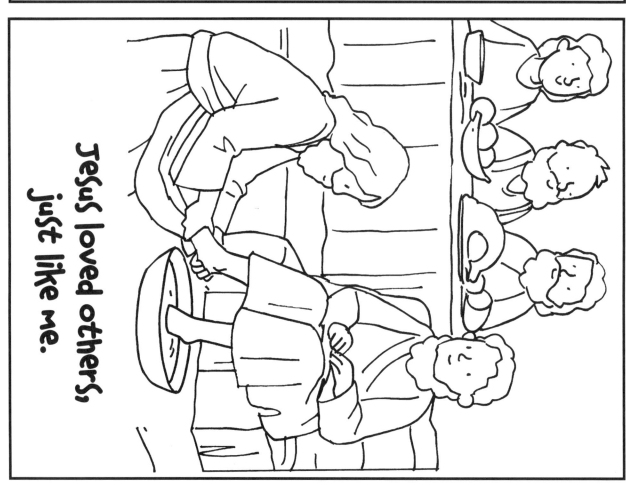

Jesus loved others,
just like me.

Jesus told others about God, just like me.

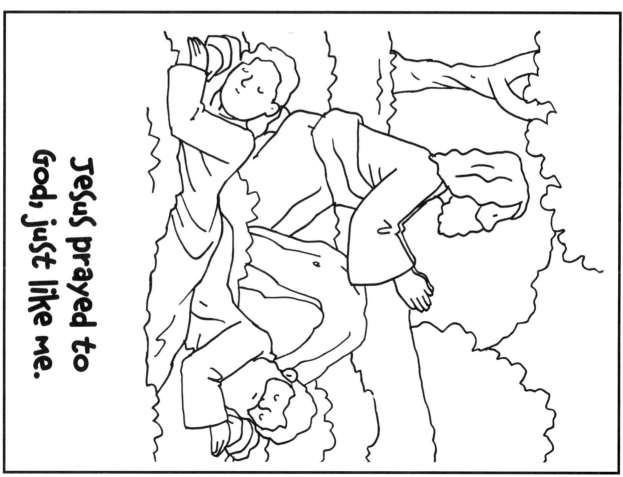

Jesus prayed to God, just like me.

Bulletin Board

What You Need

- duplicated page for each child
- stickers of Jesus

What To Do

1. Fasten an attendance chart to the bulletin board for each child. Each week, let the children place a Jesus sticker in a square

More

Attendance Chart

week 1	week 2	week 3

week 4	week 5	week 6

week 7	week 8	week 9

week 10	week 11	week 12